AF379361

O you who have believed, seek help through patience and prayer.
Indeed, Allah is with the patient {Al-Baqarah;153}

And he will provide him from (sources) he never could imagine. And whoever puts his trust in Allah, then he will suffice him. Verily, Allah will accomplish his purpose. Indeed, Allah has set a measure for all things. {Talaq;3}

So do not become weak, nor be sad, and you will be superior,
if you are indeed believers. {Al- Imran;139}

And certainly, we shall test you with something of fear, hunger, loss of wealth, lives and fruits, but give glad tidings to The Patient. {Al Baqarah;155}

Who, when afflicted with calamity, say: "Truly! to Allah we belong and truly, to him we shall return. {Al-Baqarah;156}

Allah burdens not a person greater than he can bear…
{Al-Baqarah;286}

"Our Lord! Punish us not if we forget or
fall into error..." {Al-Baqarah;286}

"You are our Maula ... (Friend, Protector, Patron, Supporter)
{Al-Baqarah;286}

..."Allah alone is enough for us, and He is the best disposer of affairs for us." {Al-Imran;173}

And He found you unaware and guided you?
{Ad-Duha; 7}

...*Unquestionably, by the remembrance of Allah hearts are assured.*

{Ar-Rad; 28}

And the next life is better for you than the first.
{Ad- Dhuha;4}

Surely with hardship comes (more) ease. {Al-Sharh; 4}

And We will surely test you with something of fear and
hunger and a loss of wealth and lives and fruits, but give good
tidings to the patient . . .

{Baqarah; 155}

O you who have believed, do not invalidate your charities with reminders … {Baqarah;264}

So let not their wealth or their children impress you. Allah only intends to punish them through them, in worldly life...
{Tawbah;55}

"And the retribution for an evil act is an evil one like it, but whoever pardons and makes reconciliation – his reward is (due) from Allah. {Ash-Shura;40}

...Indeed Allah loves those who trust in Him.

{Al-Imran;159}

If you take revenge, then do so only in proportion to the wrong done to you.
But if you bear it patiently, that is indeed best for those who are patient.
{An-Nahl;126}

If Allāh knows (any) good in your hearts, He will give you (something) better than what was taken from you.
{Anfal; 70}

Not alike are the blind and the seeing.

{Fatir;19}

Say "None can protect me from Allah's punishment, nor should I find refuge except in Him. {Jinn;22}

Oh you who believe! Whoever from among you turns back
from his religion, Allah will bring a people whom he will love
and they will love Him...{Maidah;54}

And Allah will never lead a people astray after he guided them until he makes clear to them as to what they should avoid {Taubah;115}

And the pains of childbirth drove her to the trunk of a date palm. She said, "Would that I had died before this and had been forgotten and out of sight!" {Maryum;23}

O you who have believed, Raise not your voices above the voice of the Prophet. Nor speak aloud to him in talk as you speak aloud to one another, lest your deeds may be rendered fruitless while you perceive not. {Hajj;2}

O you who believe! If a rebellious evil person comes to you
with a news, verify it, lest you harm people in ignorance,
and afterwards you become regretful to what you have done
{Hajj:6}

And if two parties or groups among believers fall to fighting,
then make peace between them both... {Hajj:9}

The believers are nothing else than brothers. So make reconciliation between your brothers, and fear Allah that you may receive mercy. {Hajj:10}

...nor let women scoff at other women, It may be that the latter are better than the former...{Hajj:11}

...nor defame one another, nor insult one another by nicknames. How bad it is to insult one another after having Iman...{Hajj:11}

And your lord creates whatsoever He wills and chooses, no choice have they in any matter (Al-Qasas-68)

And your Lord knows what their breasts conceal, and what
they reveal
(Al-Qasas;69)

It is out of your Mercy that He has put for you night and day,
that you may rest therein (during the night) and that you may
seek of his bounty (during the day) and in order that you may
be grateful {Al-Qasas 73}

And Verily! In the cattle, there is indeed a lesson for you. We give you to drink (milk) of that which is in their bellies. And there are, in them, numerous benefits for you, and of them you eat {Al-Muminun;21}

Verily, I will mislead them, and surely, I will arouse in them false desires; and certainly, I will order them to slit the ears of the cattle, and indeed I will order them to change the nature created by Allah {An-Nisa; 119}

It is He Who has created you from a single person (Adam), and (then) He has created from him his wife (Hawwa), in order that he might enjoy the pleasure of living with her… {Al-Araf;189}

It is He Who has created you from a single person (Adam),

..And that you be dutiful to your parents. If one or both of them attain old age in your life, say not to them a word of disrespect, nor shout at them but address them in terms of honor {Al-Isra;23}

For each (person), there are angels in succession, before and behind him. They guard him by the command of Allah. Verily! Allah will not change the good condition of a people as long as they do not change their state of goodness themselves... {Rad;11}